He's Risen! He's Alive!

The Story of Christ's Resurrection
Matthew 27:32–28:10 for children

Joanne E. Bader
Illustrated by Richard Heroldt

CONCORDIA PUBLISHING HOUSE • SAINT LOUIS

Jesus, our Lord, the Son of God,
Was nailed onto a cross.
And there He died on Friday eve—
His friends felt such a loss.

A few of them stood by and watched
They put Him in a tomb.
But there was nothing they could do
Their hearts were full of gloom.

Some guards were placed around the tomb.
A big stone blocked the door.
"He's all sealed in," the guards exclaimed,
"He'll be there evermore."

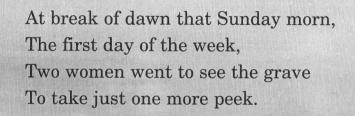

At break of dawn that Sunday morn,
The first day of the week,
Two women went to see the grave
To take just one more peek.

When Mary Magdalene got there
With another Mary,
The earth began to shake and quake.
It was very scary!

Then suddenly an angel came.
He looked as bright as day.
He shone like lightning, white as snow.
He rolled the stone away.

The guards did not know what to do.
They were afraid of him.
They shook and shook, and fell right down,
Their eyes grew very dim.

The angel sat upon the stone,
And very clearly said,
"Don't be afraid, He is not here,
He's risen from the dead."

He told the ladies, "Come and see
Where Jesus used to lay.
So you will know for sure that
He's alive this Easter day."

He spoke again, "Go quickly now,
Tell all Christ's friends that He
Has risen from the dead and will
Meet them in Galilee."

The women hastened from the tomb,
There was no time to lose.
They hurried to His disciples,
To share the awesome news.

Along the way they met a man,
It was their risen Lord.
He greeted them as they came close.
And that's when their hearts soared!

They clasped His feet and worshiped Him.
"Be not afraid," He said.
"Go tell My brothers they'll see Me
Quite soon, for I'm not dead."

Now here's what Easter's all about—
Our Jesus, He still lives!
And here's what Easter means to us—
He all our sins forgives!

Our Savior died and rose again,
For this was how God planned
To take away the sins of all
The people in the land.

He died for you, for me, for ALL,
And rose that we might live.
The gift of heav'n is ours for free
The best gift He could give.

Dear Parents,

We throw Christmas parties and birthday parties as great occasions for joy and celebration. Decorations and gifts abound. But do we place the same emphasis on our Easter celebrations?

What better party to throw than one that celebrates our risen Lord, who placed the guilt of our sins upon Himself as He carried them to the cross and rose in victory the first Easter day! Now the gift of heaven is ours for free—we do nothing to earn, it comes by grace through faith in Jesus.

Pull out all the stops this Easter and plan a celebration event. Let your children help you plan the food, decorations, and gifts. Use a large white sheet (or poster board) and permanent markers to make a party banner that reads, "He's Alive! He's Risen!" or "Jesus Is Risen!" Have your children add flowers, butterflies, and other decorations that show happiness and thanksgiving.

The Editor